# FACTS ABOUT FRENCH BULLDOGS

# FRENCH BULLDOGS HAVE ROOTS IN ENGLAND.

The French bulldog's origins are murky, but most sources trace their roots to English bulldogs. Lace makers in England were drawn to the toy version of the dog and would use the smaller pups as lap warmers while they worked. When the lace industry moved to France, they took their dogs with them. There, the English bulldogs probably bred with terriers to create bouledogues français, or French bulldogs.

# THEY WERE BRED TO BE GREAT COMPANIONS.

Frenchies are affectionate, friendly dogs that were bred to be companions. Although they're somewhat slow to be housebroken, they get along well with other dogs and aren't big barkers. The dogs don't need much exercise, so they are fine in small areas and enjoy the safety of a crate.

# THEY CAN'T SWIM.

As a result of their squat frame and bulbous head, French bulldogs can't swim, so pool owners should keep a watchful eye on their pups. Keep in mind that if you plan a beach vacation, your furry friend might feel a little left out.

# THEY MAKE GREAT BABYSITTERS.

When a baby orangutan named Malone was abandoned by his mother, the Twycross Zoo in England didn't know if he would make it. Luckily, a 9-year-old French bulldog named Bugsy stepped in and took care of the little guy. The pair became fast friends and would even fall asleep together. When Malone was big enough, he joined the other orangutans at the zoo.

# FLYING IS A PROBLEM FOR THEM, TOO.

French Bulldogs are a brachycephalic breed, meaning they have shorter snouts than other dogs. These pushed-in faces can lead to a variety of breathing problems. This facial structure, coupled with high stress and uncomfortably warm temperatures, can lead to fatal situations for dogs with smaller snouts. Many breeds like bulldogs and pugs have perished while flying, so as a result, many airlines have banned them. Luckily there are special airlines just for pets, like Pet Jets. These companies will transport dogs with special needs on their own flights separate from their owners. There's a human on board to take care of any pups that get sick or panic.

# THEY'RE SENSITIVE TO CRITICISM.

Frenchies are very sensitive, so they do not take criticism lightly. If you scold a French bulldog, it might take it very seriously and mope aroundthe house. French bulldogs respond better to positive reinforcement and encouragement.

# THEY'RE A TALKATIVE BREED.

French bulldogs might not bark much, but they do like to "talk." Using a complex system of yawns, yips, and gargles, the dogs can convey the illusion of their own language. Sometimes they will even sing along with you in the car.

# THEY HAVE TWO STYLES OF EARS.

Originally, French bulldogs had rose-shaped ears, similar to their larger relative, the English bulldog. English breeders much preferred the shape, but American breeders liked the unique bat ears. When a rose-eared bulldog was featured at the Westminster Kennel Club in 1897, American dog fanciers were very angry.

# THIS CONTROVERSY LED TO THE FORMATION OF THE FRENCH BULL DOG CLUB OF AMERICA.

The FBDCA was founded in protest of the rose-shaped ears. The organization threw its first specialty show in 1898 at New York City's famed Waldorf-Astoria. The FBDCA website described the event: "amid palms, potted plants, rich rugs and soft divans. Hundreds of engraved invitations were sent out and the cream of New York society showed up. And, of course, rose-eared dogs were not welcomed."

The somewhat catty efforts of the club led to the breed moving away from rose-shaped ears entirely. Today, French bulldogs feature the bat-shaped ears American breeders fought to showcase.

# MOST FRENCH BULLDOGS ARE BORN THROUGH ARTIFICIAL INSEMINATION.

Due to their unusual proportions, the dogs have a little trouble copulating. Males have a hard time reaching the females, and they often get overheated and exhausted when trying to get things going. As a result, a large majority of French bulldogs are created through artificial insemination. While this measure makes each litter of pups more expensive, it also allows breeders to check for potential problems during the process.

French bulldogs often also have problems giving birth, so many must undergo a C-section. The operation ensures the dog will not have to weather too much stress and prevents future health complications.

# CELEBRITIES LOVE FRENCHIES.

Frenchies make plenty of appearances in the tabloids. Celebrities like Lady Gaga, Hugh Jackman, and The Rock have all been seen frolicking with their French bulldogs. Even Leonardo DiCaprio has one—aptly named Django. Hugh Jackman's Frenchie is named Dali, after the way the dog's mouth curls like the famous artist's mustache.

# BREED CHARACT ERISTICS:

# Adaptability

Adapts Well to Apartment Living

Good For Novice Owners

Sensitivity Level

Tolerates Being Alone

Tolerates Cold Weather

Tolerates Hot Weather

# All Around Friendliness

Affectionate with Family
Incredibly Kid Friendly Dogs
Dog Friendly
Friendly Toward Strangers

# Health Grooming

- Amount Of Shedding
- Drooling Potential
- Easy To Groom
- General Health
- Potential For Weight Gain
- Size

# Trainability

Easy To Train

Intelligence

Potential For Mouthiness

Prey Drive

Tendency To Bark Or Howl

Wanderlust Potential

# Exercise
# Needs

Energy Level

Intensity

Exercise Needs

Potential For Playfulness

# HIGHLIGHTS

French Bulldogs do not need a lot of exercise, but they do need daily walks to keep them at a healthy weight.

French Bulldogs do not handle heat very well and need to be monitored on hot days to ensure that they don't overexert themselves.

French Bulldogs can be easy to train, but they can also be stubborn. Be firm and patient when training this breed.

If you value cleanliness the French Bulldog may not be the dog for you, since he is prone to drooling, flatulence and some shedding. He can also be difficult tohousetrain.

French Bulldogs can be a quiet breed and are not known as a breed that barks frequently although there are exceptions to every rule.

Because they don't tend to be excessive barkers, French Bulldogs make exceptional apartment dogs.

Although it is important to always supervise young children and dogs when they are together, the French Bulldog does very well with children.

French Bulldogs make wonderful watchdogs, but they can become territorial. They also like being the center of attention, which can lead to behavioral problems if they are overindulged.

French Bulldogs make wonderful watchdogs, but they can become territorial. They also like being the center of attention, which can lead to behavioral problems if they are overindulged.

French Bulldogs are companion dogs and thrive when they have human contact. They are not a breed that can be left alone for long periods or left outside to live.

## Size

Generally a French Bulldog is about
11 to 12 inches tall.
Males weigh 20 to 28 pounds,
females 16 to 24 pounds.

# Children
# And
# Other
# Pets

Frenchies get along well with children, and they're not so tiny
that they can't live in a household with a toddler. That said,
no dog should ever be left alone with a young child. It's just
common sense to supervise and make sure that neither is
poking or otherwise harassing the other. When they
are socialized to them during puppyhood, Frenchies can get
along well with other dogs and cats. Overly spoiled
Frenchies, however, may be jealous toward other dogs,
especially if those other dogs are getting attention from the
Frenchie's very own person.

# Feeding

Recommended daily amount: 1 to 1.5 cups of high-quality dry food a day, divided into two meals.

NOTE: How much your adult dog eats depends on his size, age, build, metabolism, and activity level. Dogs are individuals, just like people, and they don't all need the same amount of food. It almost goes without saying that a highly active dog will need more than a couch potato dog. The quality of dog food you buy also makes a difference — the better the dog food, the further it will go toward nourishing your dog and the less of it you'll need to shake into your dog's bowl.

# Health

Not all Frenchies will get any or all of these diseases, but it's important to be aware of them if you're considering this breed.

Hip Dysplasia
Brachycephalic Syndrome
Allergies
Hemivertebrae
Patellar Luxation
Intervertebral Disc Disease (IVDD)
Von Willebrand's Disease
Cleft Palate
Elongated Soft Palate

Made in United States
Orlando, FL
02 March 2022

15316057R00018

ISBN 9781093604672

9 781093 604672

# Today I'm Going Fishing with My Dad

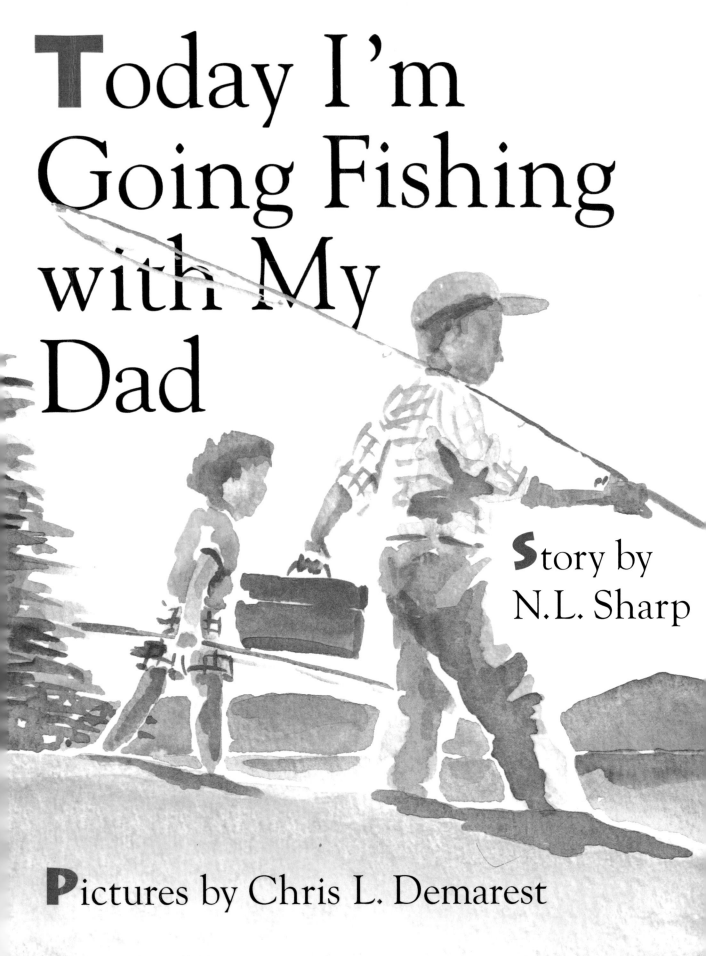

Story by
N.L. Sharp

Pictures by Chris L. Demarest